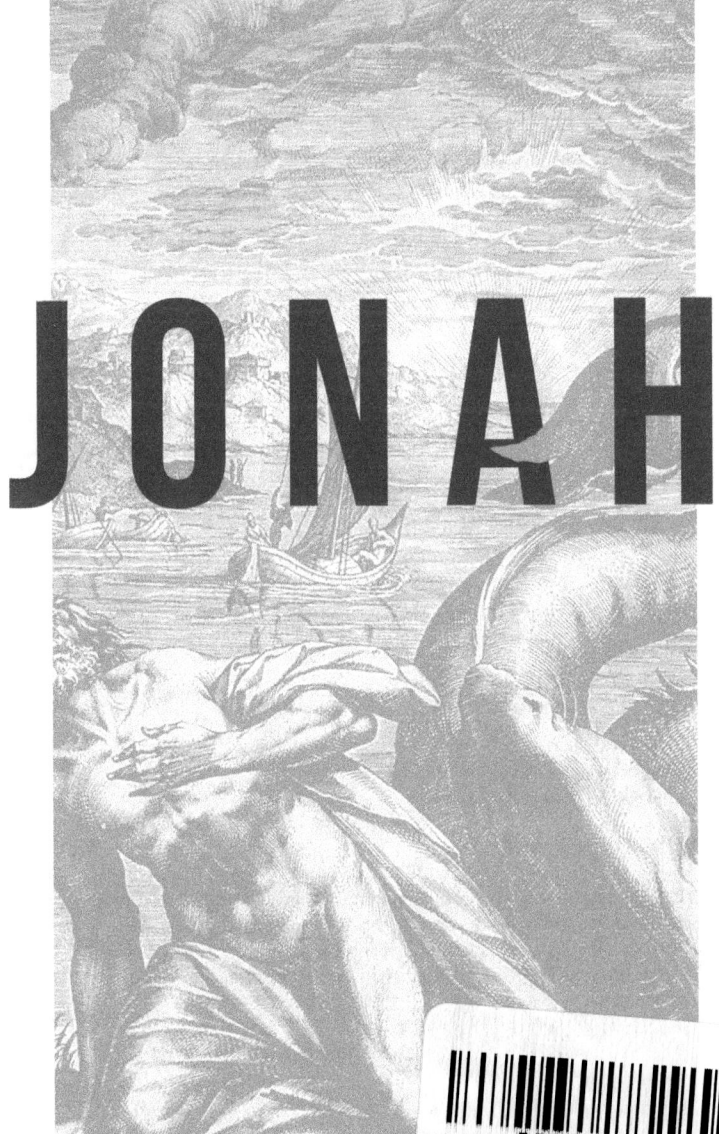

JONAH

Jonah:
Thrown into the Heart of God

Copyright © 2020 by Fontes Press

ISBN-13: 978-1-948048-52-1

All rights reserved. No part of this publication may be reproduced, stored in a retrieval system, or transmitted in any form or by any means—electronic, mechanical, photocopy, recording, or any other—except for brief quotations in printed reviews, without the prior permission of the publisher.

Cover and interior design: Midwestern Seminary Communications.

FONTES PRESS
DALLAS, TX
www.fontespress.com

A ONE MONTH VOYAGE

HOW TO USE THIS STUDY

My prayer for you is that Jesus Christ might use this little Bible study to show how He persistently pursues sinners with a capacity for mercy that is deeper than the seas. We see over and over again on the pages of Scripture that the Lord often sees fit to set His divine sights upon sinners for His saving purposes…and He never fails to hit His target. The point: He delights to save sinners from all walks of life.

First, this study is designed to provide the reader with brief comments and background information to aid in the task of grasping the meaning of the book of Jonah. The "Points to Ponder" sections are meant to provoke you to a greater understanding of who the Lord is and how you can more pleasingly live under His kindly rule.

Second, this little study comes with a small challenge attached to it. I call it the 4-1-4 challenge. You ready? …I challenge you to read a chapter of Jonah every day for four weeks in a row. Here's how it works: Week one you read Jonah 1 every day. Then, in sequence, you do the same by reading Jonah two during week two. Simple enough, right? I have designed this challenge in hopes to bring your heart into maximum impact with the kind heart of the Lord through His written text—the Bible, plain and simple.

SAMUEL BIERIG
Dean of Spurgeon College

WEEK 1

JONAH 1	MONDAY	TUESDAY	WEDNESDAY	THURSDAY	FRIDAY	SATURDAY	SUNDAY

WEEK 2

JONAH 2	MONDAY	TUESDAY	WEDNESDAY	THURSDAY	FRIDAY	SATURDAY	SUNDAY

WEEK 3

JONAH 3	MONDAY	TUESDAY	WEDNESDAY	THURSDAY	FRIDAY	SATURDAY	SUNDAY

WEEK 4

JONAH 4	MONDAY	TUESDAY	WEDNESDAY	THURSDAY	FRIDAY	SATURDAY	SUNDAY

SETTING

MAIN THEMES

- The Lord is gracious, compassionate, slow to anger, rich in loyalty and love, and does not delight in the destruction of sinners (4:2)
- The Lord saves unlikely people in unlikely ways (2:9; 3:10)
- The Lord is merciful to the merciless (1:14, 17; 3:10)
- The Lord is a missionary (1:2; 3:2)
- The Lord is patient with sinners (1:17; 3:10; 4:10-11)
- The Lord expects repentance (1:15-16; 3:1-3, 4; pay particular attention to 4:10-11)
- The Lord judges those who oppose Him (2:4)

AUTHORSHIP

- We do not know who the final compiler of the material that comprises Jonah was. However, Jonah is the most likely author of the details and narrative elements as he was a firsthand witness. Therefore, the Holy Spirit orchestrated that the final author of the book remains anonymous.

DATE

- The most probable date for Jonah's life and ministry is the eight century BC. Jonah's ministry took place during the reign of King Jeroboam II, who was in power from 782-753 BC. Since we do not really know who wrote the book of Jonah, the most precise date we can put on the time the book was written is somewhere between 800 B.C. and 300 B.C.

ASSYRIA

- The Assyrian empire was the undisputed superpower of the world for nearly three hundred years (911 BC-612 BC). When conquering a culture, people, or city, the Assyrians were swift, punishing, and barbaric. They were renowned for their brutal tactics, which they amply applied to soldier and civilian alike. By advanced siege towers, ramps, and scaling ladders, the Assyrians would crush their opposition. They were known to snatch enemy fighters off the city walls and then skin them alive before terrorized onlookers. They would sever limbs and rip out tongues. They would skewer city officials on poles. They were even known to disembowel pregnant women, thereby killing both mother and child by the most heinous means imaginable. I do not linger over the Assyrian's ruthlessness for any reason but to attune the reader to the character of the people to whom Jonah was called (1:1-2). Knowledge of Assyria's cruelty does not lessen Jonah's guilt, but it does allow a degree of resonance with Jonah when we read.

GEOGRAPHY

- When Jonah receives the word of the Lord to preach to Nineveh (1:2), he promptly and abruptly disobeys by going in the exact opposite direction. He strikes out from the Northern Kingdom of Israel by traveling southwestward toward Joppa and eventually Tarshish. Jonah's physical, geographical descent is meant to be taken as a nearly precise shadow of the reality of his disobedient, sinful descent away from the presence of the Lord! Our author wishes to sweep us up into a vivid and ironic portrayal of Jonah's disobedience and its consequences. As Jonah descends downward geographically, he descends downward morally as well. Jonah's geographical choices serve as a kind of real-time representation for his moral descent and allow the reader to observe that descent. After boarding a vessel in the seafaring city of Joppa, he sails west for Tarshish. Although we do not know the precise location of the ancient city of Tarshish, it is clear our author intends to depict Jonah as sprinting, sailing, swimming, sinking, and all-out sinning his way as far from God's presence as possible. Tarshish was likely located somewhere in modern-day Spain and lay on the outer perimeter of the known world.

NINEVEH

What was once the ancient city of Nineveh is now the modern-day city of Mosul, Iraq (near Baghdad). At the time of Jonah's ministry, Nineveh was the capital of the Assyrian empire and was likely the leading commercial center of Assyria. And as we read in 4:11, the city boasted a population of 120,000 citizens.

CHAPTER ONE

SWALLOWED UP IN GOD'S DEPTHLESS MERCY

ACT 1, SCENE 1: JONAH, THE AMAZINGLY DISOBEDIENT PROPHET OF GOD (VV.1-3)

1:1

Jonah was the son of Amittai (see 2 Kings 14:25 and the authorship and date sections above).

1:2-3

God tells Jonah to do three things:

1) "Get up" or "arise"
2) "Go"
3) "Preach" or "proclaim"

Jonah, seemingly without even flinching, disobeys by going in the exact opposite direction. He gets up, but he does not "get up" and "go" to Nineveh. Instead, Jonah goes "down" (1:2; 1:3; 1:5). Instead of "going" to Nineveh he goes southwest to Joppa. Instead of preaching the Lord's message, Jonah attempts to silently sprint ("flee") from the presence of the Lord—a futile attempt as he himself confesses in 1:9 ("I'm a Hebrew. I worship the Lord, the God of the heavens, who made the sea and the dry land.").

Jonah was in the Northern Kingdom of Israel and therefore traveled south ("down") to the city of Joppa, which is the opposite of what the Lord told him to do (1:1.) He was told to go northeast to Nineveh. The author of Jonah is intentionally portraying Jonah as oppositional and defiant. He boards a boat and travels west toward Tarshish, which was likely in present day Spain. Jonah was sprinting and sailing his way toward the end of the known world in hopes of escaping the presence of the Lord.

THE DECEPTIVE PROMISE OF DISOBEDIENCE

When we are in the midst of our sin, really in the throes of it, there is no quicker forgotten (ignored?) attribute of God than His omnipresence. What Jonah conveniently forgets is that God is all-present. There is no corner of the universe where our triune God is not inhabiting His creation with His glory.

This is key for understanding Jonah's story.

What does the doctrine of God's omnipresence (all-present) mean for you and me when we are pursuing hard after our sin?

ACT 1, SCENE 2: THE PERFECT STORM (VV.4-15)

1:4

What is fascinating about v.4 is that God Himself is the one who throws the great storm atop the seas. This storm shows that the Lord is not only all-present, but that He is also all-powerful. The Lord, and the Lord alone, is uniquely capable of causing the winds and the rains to swirl about Jonah's fragile little boat in such a way as to make it threaten "to break apart." The language here is very vivid. Because of the storm, the boat responds by threatening to come apart.

JESUS: THE ALL-PRESENT, ALL-POWERFUL GOD OF ALL UNIVERSES

Turn over to the New Testament book of Mark and read 4:35-41. After you read through the whole story, write down all the similarities and parallels you see between that story and what you find in Jonah 1:4-16.

1. _____

2. _____

3. _____

4. _____

5. _____

1:5-6

These sailors were polytheists. That means they worshiped many false gods. They begin to call upon these many false (and powerless!) gods to save them. Meanwhile, Jonah continues to descend further down into the bowels of the boat—still seeking to escape the eye of God, the all-present One. This is, of course, a futile endeavor.

It is important to note that the sailors were calling out to and praying to "gods" in general. In the story, there is a very stark contrast between the generic gods of the sailors (elohim) and the Lord of Jonah (Yahweh, 1:1, 9). We should take note that when God puts His divine power on display by calming the storm in 1:15, the pagan sailors respond with an overwhelming sense of fear toward the God of Jonah (Yahweh, 1:16).

1:7-9

The Lord is shown to even control the roll of dice ("lots"). He perfectly works this act of supposed chance to land on Jonah.

If there was ever a golden opportunity for a Hebrew to share the good news of the Lord's salvation for sinners, this was it! These sailors are compelled by their dire circumstances to inquire further about Jonah's vocation, homeland, and ethnic descent. He responds by professing that he serves the Lord of all life and creation, the God of Israel.

So it is! Even through the strangest of circumstances, Jonah still winds up "preaching" (1:2) as the Lord had commanded him. His answer is true and somewhat comical. He confesses the folly of his own plan as he confesses to running from God on the very land God created, upholds, and controls. He confesses further that he is attempting to sail away from the presence of the Lord of the seas on the very sea that the Lord created, upholds, and controls!

Jonah's confession is charged with worship language. He says, "I fear the Lord" or "I worship the Lord," meaning he worships, reveres, and abides by the precepts of this Lord of land and sea.

1:10-11

By this point the sailors are beginning to connect the dots between Jonah's disobedience, God's unmistakable response, and their now looming doom! They are now, surprisingly, not angry and frightened for their lives!

The storm is becoming more and more deadly. It is increasing in intensity with every passing minute. This reality confirms and amplifies the sailors' need to purge the vessel of Jonah.

1:12-13

Jonah says, "I know that I'm to blame for this great storm that is against you." It does not seem, however, that Jonah is repentant in any way. At this point he has merely resigned himself to the unavoidability of divine judgment. Jonah has accepted his imminent judgment, and as the resident expert on the Lord of Lords, the sailors have turned to him to ask advice on how to appease the Lord Almighty. From this, we might glean that there is always retribution for sin. Either you pay the price for your sin eternally in hell, or Jesus Christ pays for your sin on the cross. There is no middle or other way. Jonah, then, serves best in the landscape of the Bible as an example of what not to do—how not to follow Jesus.

We would be wise to take note of Jonah's lack of repentance here. This is emblematic of what we will see confirmed later in 4:2 when he says, "Isn't this what I thought while I was in my own country? That's why I fled toward Tarshish in the first place." In other words, in 1:12 we are not observing a repentant Jonah but rather a stubbornly disobedient Jonah. And aren't we often just like him?

These sailors are shown—even as pagans—to take far more care and show more mercy for Jonah than he does for them. Their lives are in jeopardy, and yet they do all in their power to save him. And this after he had resigned to let them dispose of him. This aspect of the story shows just how off course Jonah had become. He cared so very little for the eternal suffering of the Ninevites and these sailors in particular.

HE ANSWERED THEM, "I'M A HEBREW. I WORSHIP YAHWEH, THE GOD OF THE HEAVENS, WHO MADE THE SEA AND THE DRY LAND."

IS GOD A GOOD JUDGE?

Why must God punish disobedience? The Lord expects holiness and obedience from His creatures/creation. Does that bother you? (See 1:9.)

Would God be a righteous judge if He lets murderers, liars, rapists, disrespecters of parents, fornicators, gluttons, etc., off the hook? How does Jesus' death on the cross in the place of sinners solve this problem?

Do you ever respond to God's discipline like Jonah did? Do you sometimes dig your heels in and act as though you know better than God, or do you humble yourself, confess, and turn from your disobedience?

How and where are you currently living in disobedience? Are you in a sexually immoral relationship? What would your internet search history tell us? Are you living for the glory of the world through sports, popularity, or straight A's?

What is your plan for turning away from your particular sins and false idols?

1:14-15

This is an amazing prayer and act of faith on behalf of these sailors. Imagine yourself in their situation! A storm threatens to engulf, or at least capsize, your ship...you are making ready to throw a passenger overboard to certain doom...and now you are asked to grab this man's arms and legs and assist in throwing him overboard...you're about to heave him onto the wiles of the stormy seas. And then you look up to the heavens to pray to a God you barely believe in...rain and tears are mixing and then streaming down your cheeks, your clothes drenched, lightning and thunder are cracking all about you. These sailors were really in this scenario!

They beseeched God, asking for two things:

1. "Please Lord, don't let us perish because of this man's life.
2. And don't charge us with innocent blood!"

Then they professed:
"For you, Lord, have done just as you pleased."

Due to God's divine judgment still looming over Jonah, these sailors have changed their generic understanding of gods in general (1:5), to now distinguishing Him as the Lord of all—Lord of land, sea, and every creature. They respond to the Lord's divine intervention by confessing, "You, Lord, have done just as you pleased." This Lord (Yahweh), whom they have providentially slammed into upon the tumultuous seas, is distinctively and absolutely sovereign—undefeated and undefeatable.

ACT 1, SCENE 3: GOD'S MERCIFUL AQUATIC VEHICLE OF MIRACULOUS PROPORTIONS

1:16

The "fear" and awe these men first felt in 1:10, as Jonah explains his origins, is now confirmed and even accentuated. The seas stop their raging, thus validating the truth of the words of the prophet of the Lord. Jonah prophesied that the Lord would relinquish His will to rage against them if they would but cast him out into the severity of the seas. The sailors do so, and Jonah's prophecy is confirmed. If you were a sailor on this particular vessel, this would confirm the god-ness of Jonah's God for you.

1:17

It is more significant for our author's intent to recognize that the fish is obedient to God than it is to note the sensational nature of a fish swallowing Jonah. What is being highlighted is that the sea, the sailors, the boat, and now the fish all obey God's command. But not Jonah! Jonah is the lone rebel amidst the characters in the book of Jonah. Nonetheless, we are remiss if we fail to pause over the nearly incomprehensible nature of the Lord's ability, skill, and astounding wisdom in appointing this monstrous fish to engulf Jonah. This is a masterfully designed, fleshy submarine, built to be the exact vehicle of the Lord's merciful deliverance. This fish has the unique task of bringing Jonah safely back to the shore.

God's astounding mercy is on full display at this point in the story. God seeks to reach down with a bottomless mercy now to scoop up the merciless city of Nineveh. And He chose the merciless Jonah to preach that message. The Lord heaps up mercy on top of mercy for Jonah, Nineveh, and the sailors. Jonah, though, returns these kindnesses with rebellion. Not one to be bested, the Lord yet pursues Jonah's rebel heart all the way to the sea bottom of his sin!

Jonah has come to the bottom (the ocean bottom!) of his downward, rebellious descent (see 1:3, 5). It is at these last depths of Jonah's descent, the precise moment of his greatest vulnerability and complete lack of power, that God mercifully swallows him up in His mercy. This is meant to teach us that even at our sinful depths, fathoms deep though they are, that God saves sinners. It is at the far reaches of all our raging that God shows up. He is not unaware, not embarrassed, intimidated, or deterred by our depravity. No, He shows up as the kindhearted, confident King of the universe, utterly unlike the despots and dictators this world has known. He steps down off His throne, as it were, and runs us down—swims after us even! He relentlessly pursues us. He never stops! He won't stop! He can't stop chasing after those He has set His love on to save.

God goes to such lengths to kindly conquer our sin-prone hearts that sending a colossal fish to swallow us up in His love is not even out of the bounds. Just as we are helplessly flailing about with our last energies, burning the last of our calories, choking upon the icy waters of our sin, gasping for our last, He yet comes to get us. Jonah hates God, and still He comes. Jonah is in such state, weakened by fatigue, that he cannot fight God's mercy. God overtakes him, swallows him up in the good news of His grace.

BRINGING IT ALL TOGETHER

Can anyone or anything outrun the presence of God?

Who or what is Tarshish in your life—that thing that you run to, hoping that it will give you at least the hope of the so-called "good life" you are chasing?

Who or what is Nineveh for you? How are you avoiding God?

Did you know that no matter what you have done in your past—even if you have lived in ultimate defiance of God like Jonah—God can and will forgive you when you turn from your sin and put your whole life, all of your trust, in God? That means, you give Him your relationships, social media accounts, money, dreams, everything.

Jonah serves best as a negative example for us. Why is that?
Look at 1:12 for the answer.
He isn't even repentant.

Did you know that no matter what you have done in your past, God can still use you?

How does God respond to Jonah's defiance? Does He show up as a tyrant, or as merciful and benevolent?

Is the fish an act of judgment or mercy?

CHAPTER TWO

JONAH'S PRAYER

ACT 2, SCENE 1: GOD HEARS JONAH (VV.1-10)

2:1

When the sailors toss Jonah overboard, he is delivered—shockingly!—from a certain, watery grave. He is, as it were, swallowed up in the mercy of God—saved away by God's vehicle of rescue. And it is there, from the belly of the fish that Jonah voices a prayer of thanksgiving and praise, but interestingly it does not seem to be a prayer of regret or remorse over his disobedience. We should take notice that this is the first time in the story that Jonah prays.

2:2

Jonah prayerfully recounts his desperation and how he cried out to the Lord from the prison of the underworld, as it seemed to him, at least that is how he experienced it. His prayerful declaration is that God heard his cry and delivered him from a watery grave.

2:3

Jonah professes that the Lord is the ultimate influence behind his predicament. But I thought the sailors threw Jonah into the sea? Well, the psychological tension we feel between God's sovereignty and man's agency is no tension at all in the book of Jonah. He understands that the real 'muscle on the move' to bring him to safety is God.

Jonah testifies to his state: "The current overcame me. All your breakers and your billows swept over me." Through his prayer, we can see Jonah coming to terms with the kindness of the Lord—even amidst his many fears. Jonah is beginning to recognize the kindness and smiling providence of God in His sending the storm and the fish.

GOD RELENTLESSLY PURSUES SINNERS

It is impossible for God to act or to be contrary to His nature. And His nature is to deliver mutineers like Jonah. He relentlessly pursues Jonah. He will stop at almost nothing to pull, prod, and propel Jonah toward obedience. God is good, and He will not leave Jonah outside of His good and fatherly care.

Have you ever seen how something painful in your life—even a time when you were disobedient—proved to be the smiling providence of God? Maybe it was a time when you could not tell on the surface level, but God was making a masterpiece. He was teaching you about Himself and in the process of the pain, He was giving you more of Himself.

2:4

In this verse we see the poetic irony of Jonah's story. In chapter one Jonah wanted nothing more than to escape the face of God (1:3), but when he finally succeeds, he hates it! As the verse continues he further testifies to his vulnerability and God's kind mercy. Jonah does not shy away from his weakness.

Out floating on those deathly waters, Jonah felt the sting of Lord's disapproval.

It must have been a crushing blow. It was a banishment with purpose, though. God never wastes our hurt. The Lord was using quite extreme measures to wake Jonah from his sinful trance. And Jonah responds with the strong hope that he will again look long toward the temple of God. Even though he is experiencing the discipline of the Lord, he knows that salvation will come from no other place than the Lord. God is both afflictor and deliverer in our story. It is the Lord Himself who has chosen to afflict Jonah, and it is the Lord who will rescue him.

JESUS: THE TRUE, BETTER, AND GREATER JONAH

Jesus too was once banished from the Lord's presence (Matt 27:45-50 and Psalm 22). But He was not guilty of sin! Jonah was driven out because of his sin, but Jesus was driven out on behalf of sinners. He Himself was sinless!

Consider the following parallels between Jesus and Jonah:

- Jonah hates Nineveh and responds with anger < Jesus loved Jerusalem and wept over her

- Jonah delighted to preach destruction to Nineveh < Jesus delighted to preach forgiveness by His blood

- Jonah is full of sin, yet the Father mercifully spared him < Jesus had no sin, yet died like a sinner to deliver sinners like you and me

- Jonah was in the belly of the fish and figuratively arose from the heart of the seas after three days, thus was a foreshadowing < Jesus got up out of the belly of the earth after three days and was the substance

2:5-7

Jonah was to "get up" and go to Nineveh in 1:1-3, but here in 2:5-6 we see he has reached the finality of his descent. He has sprinted, sailed, swum, and sunk his way as far south as the world will physically allow. He reached the bottom of the seas in his efforts to run from the Lord's presence (1:3).

At this point in the story, Jonah is writing with the whole of the episode in his rearview mirror, as it were. The belly of the fish in no longer his aquatic jail cell. His prayer is a poetic recounting of his psychological state just before he is rescued by the fish. His thankfulness breaks forth at the point of rescue. God did not leave him nor forsake him but met him where he was.

Notice the word "remembered" in verse 7. Jonah realizes at the end of his rebellious descent that there is no other person by whom he can be saved (cf. 2:9). Jonah's hope rests on a God who hears him.

GOD HEARS YOU

This is where the Lord reaches out to many of us—when our muscles have no more calories to burn in efforts of a self-salvation plan, when we've tread the waters of our disobedience long enough, and Jesus comes and swallows us up in mercy just as we are drowning in all our sins.

Is your story like this?

Are you currently running in the direction of disobedience? It is important to remember that Jesus hears you (Micah 7:7)!

2:8-9

From the innards of a colossal, God-appointed, Mediterranean fish, Jonah offers up a sacrifice of thanksgiving and a voice of praise. There isn't much one will find to sacrifice in that kind of place, is there? But, the Lord is ever seeking a heart bent toward Him, and He mercifully honors Jonah's misguided prayer. He is still holding onto his self-righteousness, but there is a flicker of humility in him, and his kind Lord works with that.

Jonah offers the only two worldviews available: (1) Loyalty to Yahweh, (2) Loyalty to empty idols. Jonah's point is that loyalty to powerless idols will not save as Yahweh has saved here. Jonah's heart is toward Nineveh now. He isn't excited about it, but it does seem that he turned to vow his life in pledge.

"Salvation belongs to the Lord" is one of the key themes of Jonah. This is an unqualified statement for Jonah. But, as we should sense, Jonah's actions seem to put to the test his belief that he himself is his own savior. This is what we see in 4:2. Jonah does not see himself as an object of God's mercy so much as he sees himself as a righteous man.

DID JONAH REPENT?

Notice the absence of confession and repentance in Jonah's prayer. Jonah still has a self-righteous tone in his voice as he prays. He is theologically correct, but his heart is more that of a person who needs no savior. "No mercy needed here, Lord!" says Jonah.

Is there a little bit of Jonah inside of you? Jonah is as a mirror for our own lives. We also are quite capable of seeing ourselves as quite righteous—as if we are in little need of the Lord's grace and mercy!

2:10

Note that the fish obeys God in his appointment to swallow Jonah, and when he is commanded to vomit Jonah onto the shore, he again promptly obeys.

The fish is meant to be an instrument of mercy and humiliation. It seems that Jonah did not receive either in the fullest sense that the Lord meant for him to 'get it.' Jonah ends his prayer still holding onto his pride and very much seeing himself as far more deserving of God's kindnesses than the Ninevites and pagan sailors are.

In Matthew 12:38-42 the scribes and Pharisees are yet again badgering Jesus for signs and wonders to prove His deity. Jesus suspends their questions and diverts them by pointing them to the "sign of Jonah." It seems Jesus has in mind His eventual death and burial in, and resurrection from, the belly of the earth as the evidential sign they will be given. Jesus seems to mean this in at least two ways: (1) Nineveh received no miracles, only preaching. Thus, Jesus came to preach, and if the scribes and Pharisees do not believe Jesus at His preaching, why would a trick here and there turn their spiritually dead hearts into beating ones? (2) He means to point ultimately to His cross and resurrection as the ultimate sign. What greater sign is there than the Son of God conquering death? By way of the resurrection, Jesus has firmly placed His boot on death's neck!

A FATHER WHO WOUNDS TO ULTIMATELY HEAL

When Jonah is swimming in the mirk and mire of his sin and rebellion, sitting under the discipline of the Lord, it would have been difficult to "feel" God's love and mercy. But it was never more present, was it? It is just the same with God's children now. He often wounds to heal.

Read Romans 8:31-39 for perspective:

8:31-32 Will He grant His children nothing?
8:33 Can any devil or man-centered court bring accusation against His children?
8:34 Does God condemn you?
8:35 Who can separate us from the love of God? No one.
8:37 Are you destined to be vanquished or victorious over your sin and condemnation? Jesus has conquered sin, death, and the devil on your behalf!
8:38 What could keep us from the love of God? Nothing!
8:39 Who or what stands to condemn you? No one and no thing.

CHAPTER THREE

JONAH'S PREACHING

ACT 3, SCENE 1: JONAH SORT OF OBEYS (VV.1-3)

3:1-3

The fish vomits Jonah on to the shore (2:10), and Jonah is told to (1) "Get up!" (2) "Go" (3) "Preach." Jonah is given the same "word" to deliver to "Nineveh...an extremely great city, a three-day walk." However, this time Jonah actually goes and preaches according to the Lord's command. Notice that chapter 3 intentionally mirrors the same three commands as Jonah 1:1-3. In the Lord's kindness and mercy, Jonah receives a second chance, and consequently, so do the Ninevites.

The author tells us that "Nineveh was an extremely great city, a three-day walk." This most likely refers to Nineveh as a sprawling metropolis.

ACT 3, SCENE 2: GOD'S WORD IS ENOUGH (VV.4-9)

3:4

Colin Smith says, "At the heart of Jonah's story is the remarkable account of how a pagan city was transformed by the preaching of God's Word." You must keep this at the forefront of your mind as you read this remarkable story. The book of Jonah is not so much about Jonah, the Ninevites, or even the great fish—it's about the kindhearted mercy of the Lord toward sinners. So, again, as you read, do not get distracted by the fish, the wind, the waves, and the miraculous plant. These are essential elements of the story, but they are not primary. The author intends us to remain focused on God's character and His astounding power in turning the hearts of some 120,000 brutal, undeserving people...and this at the mere spoken word of a backslidden prophet!

God does not need strobe lights, smoke machines, and a 'killer band' to do His work! No, the Lord works through the preaching of His Word, and He often does so in quite simple ways just as here in Jonah chapter three. If you will commit to reading and hearing God's Word, eternal fruit will be produced in you (Isaiah 55:10-11). That is the promise we find in Jonah chapter three.

Jonah's sermon is stingingly short and pointed: "In forty days Nineveh will be demolished!" Whatever else Jonah might have preached, our author is intentionally showcasing Jonah's faithfulness to the message the Lord conveyed to him. We take Jonah's message to be faithful to God's Word by observing three things: (1) In 1:2 the Lord makes it clear that He intended Jonah to preach a message "against" Nineveh. In other words, it was to be a message of God's opposition. (2) We are to infer that Jonah would have included the same basic information about the Lord and what repentance is as he did with the sailors in 1:9. (3) The previous point is further informed by the Ninevites' response in 3:5-9. The author intends for his reader to read the response/repentance of the Ninevites as being informed by the information provided in Jonah's preached message. They therefore fast, put on sackcloth, and "turn" from their "evil ways."

Yet, at this point in the narrative, we are climbing the steep hill of the climax of the story, which takes place in 4:2. Yes, Jonah is faithful to his vow (2:9), but he hates every moment of it. Jonah is beginning to detect the Lord's intentions. He smells what the Lord is cooking up, and he does not like it. Jonah knows that the Lord sends "word" of warning when He means to bring a people to Himself in repentance.

3:5

Jonah 3:5 presents all of us with a strong witness for the astounding power of God to turn a wicked heart. Sinclair Ferguson says, "Of course, it follows that they must have believed Jonah, but they did not feel that it was the voice of Jonah they heard." What is the point? Jonah was no great orator! Rather, God is a great God, mighty in mercy and grace. That is the point of the book. God set His sights on the citizens of Nineveh, and He never misses His target. The Ninevites heard the voice of the one true and living God that day despite the cold, calculated words of Jonah. They turned from their sins!

3:6

Even the king of Nineveh repents! By stepping down from his throne and taking off his kingly garb, he is signaling his submission to the Lord of all creation (cf. 1:9).

3:7-9

These verses portray a vision of total corporate repentance. The people cut off food as well as water. This is a total fast. These drastic measures signal the depth of remorse the king and citizens feel. They sense the danger of the looming destruction, and they respond accordingly as they are cut to the heart. Notice that even the animals fast.

The primary way we turn from our sins is to turn from our 'ways'—our patterns—our habits, systems of evil, corruption, and sin.

Your friend or even fellow church member is not loving if he or she does not confront you in your sins? No, he is no friend who does not aggressively attack sin in his fellow image bearer! The most loving thing anyone could ever do is to seek to eliminate the sin habits of others. A true friend is someone who would risk losing respect, sentiment, and even friendship in pursuit of cutting out sin from the life of another. That kind of friend will speak truth even when it is painful. God knows that sin is like a quick-moving cancer that will eventually bring you down to eternal death. If you go all in with a life of sin, you will never recover—even in eternity.

HOW DO YOU RESPOND TO GOD'S WORD?

1. Is your response like Jonah's in chapter one? Have you run away from Him and lived in disobedience?

2. Were you once reluctant to obey like Jonah, but now you have turned to the Lord and believed Him at His Word? How is your life different now than it used to be when you lived in disobedience?

3. Is your response to God's call of obedience like the Ninevites here in chapter 3? Do you consistently believe Jesus at His Word and turn from your sin in the lasting sense?

ACT 3, SCENE 3: HE DID NOT DO IT (V.10)

3:10

First, this verse puts the Lord's merciful heart on full display. The Lord's heart does not reflex toward punishment but toward pardon. It has been said that God's merciful posture toward sinners sits permanently on a hair-trigger, but His judgment He keeps locked away, only reverting to such measures when absolutely necessary. In other words, He is willing and more than ready to unload oceans full of mercy on sinners but is patient and quite reluctant in unleashing His judgment (i.e., the doctrine of hell). This is what we see so entrenched in God's nature when Peter says, "The Lord does not delay His promise, as some understand delay, but is patient with you, not wanting any to perish but all to come to repentance" (2 Peter 3:9).

Second, this verse does not exemplify a God who changes His mind, but rather is meant to highlight how intimately and personally involved the Lord is in the repentance and rebellion of every single person who has ever walked this earth. We are to think of it similarly to how a non-repentant sinner sits under the looming judgment of God until the moment he turns from his sin in trust toward God in

Christ. His position before God has now changed. Had he
remained in his sins, he would have rightfully received God's
wrath, but he does not because he has turned from his sin.
Similarly, Jonah's message of warning is the means by which
God brings about the repentance of the Ninevites. He does
not change His mind in the sense that a man does, rather, this
is the veiled will of God now on full display. In the providence
and secret council of the Trinity, this was always the plan.
This is precisely why Jonah was so upset—because it is often
at the warning of judgment that people repent, as it was
with Nineveh! The preaching was the means of the eventual
believing and turning (Romans 10:14-16).

GOD SAVES WHOMEVER HE PLEASES!

In Jonah 3 we see that the Lord turns thousands upon
thousands of people away from their sins and toward a new
life in Himself.

What does this teach us about people who may seem to
be beyond salvation?

Who are the people in your life that you need to share the
good news of the forgiveness they can find in Jesus' death in
their place on the cross? Name one or two people and decide
today to make a plan for how you intend to share the good
news with them.

In chapter one our author expresses the southward descent of
Jonah as a kind of visible analogy for his downward spiritual
descent, a spiral, if you will. He is running and sailing as fast
as possible from God's presence (1:3). God blows something
to the effect of a category 3 hurricane onto the seas and every

life aboard the ship is imperiled. The chapter ends in semi-climactic fashion as the sailors on Jonah's getaway ship throw him onto the wiles of the seas—at Jonah's own word. God appoints a miraculous fish to swallow Jonah and then deliver him safely back to the shore. The picture is that of being swallowed up, completely enveloped in the judgment of God. But in 1:17 there is a greater picture emerging: a picture of a relentless God, a God who will not leave nor forsake Jonah to die in his sins. The fish was God's rescue mission, and though we are accustomed to talking about the hands and feet of God, in Jonah's case it seems God came to get a sinner by way of fins and gills. Jonah is swallowed up whole in the bottomless ocean of God's mercy.

In chapter two we catch up with Jonah while in the bowels of the aquatic beast. Up to this point Jonah has run, sailed, swum, and sunk his way as far from God's presence as possible—he had sinned his way to the bottom of the sea. It is here, in the belly of the beast, that Jonah belches his sing-song prayer of thanksgiving. He finally relents his pride. He gives testimony that at rock bottom seafloor where he thought he could outrun and outsink God's mercy, he finds out he cannot. Even at the bottom, God is there. Jonah prays a prayer of hope and praise.

In chapter three Jonah has finally decided to obey God's call on his life—halfhearted obedience though it was. He delivers the Lord's message of destruction, and Nineveh responds with unprecedented trust and repentance. In verse ten the Lord is said to have observed their repentance, and He, even more miraculous than the Ninevites salvation, responds by diverting away from His disaster He "threatened." This leads us into chapter four where we find a now enraged Jonah.

CHAPTER FOUR

JONAH'S ANGER

ACT 4, SCENE 1: THE DEFINITION OF GOD (VV.1-4)

4:1-2

Jonah does not want to live in a world where brutal and grotesque evildoers like the Ninevites get off the hook. He would rather live in a world where wicked people like the Ninevites get what they 'deserve.' He says in effect, "All the way back in Israel I knew you were like this, Lord! You can't help Yourself! And I just did not want to see it happen. I knew You were going to turn the heart of these vicious people."

Jonah wanted to see the Ninevites burn—literally! He wanted to see God rain down heavenly fire and fury just like He did at Sodom and Gomorrah (Genesis 19). And you must remember that God would be completely just if He had chosen to do so! When you pursue your sin, God is ethically just in destroying you right there on the spot. This is what makes the sacrifice of Jesus on the cross in the stead of sinners so transcendentally wonderful. Jesus, in His strength, chose to show up as mercy instead of fury.

Jonah lost sight of just how sinful he himself is. Somehow in the deepest, darkest recesses of his heart Jonah saw himself as different. Somewhere along the way he began to see himself as superior to others, and the Ninevites were just the starkest example of this false vision of himself. In Jonah's vision of himself he was somehow less needy of the Lord's mercy and compassion than others. Jonah was cut from the cloth of those respectable types—you know, the kind of people who are cleaned up. In our day this is the suburban types, the folks with insurance and white-collar desk jobs, church-goers even...depending on your region. Jonah's personal guilt and sin-nature had somehow been eclipsed in his vision of himself.

After all the miracles, mercies, and saving, Jonah still could not see his need. He probably still stank of God's mercies manifest through the gallons of ocean water and the bile of belly of the fish. Jonah had misconstrued it all. This is the tragedy of our sin, too! Sin is incredibly blinding. Jonah no longer saw himself in desperate need of the mercies and grace of God, all the while being a recipient of the same mercy that he is scorning in God.

Jonah had certainly read Genesis 19 and even hoped that God would destroy Nineveh as he did Sodom and Gomorrah, but I wonder why he so conveniently forgot what happens just a few books later in the Bible in Deuteronomy 7:1-8:

> "1When the Lord your God brings you into the land you are entering to possess, and he drives out many nations before you—the Hittites, Girgashites, Amorites, Canaanites, Perizzites, Hivites and Jebusites, seven nations more numerous and powerful than you—2and when the Lord your God delivers them over to you and you defeat them, you must completely destroy them. Make no treaty with them and show them no mercy. 3You must not intermarry with them, and you must not give your daughters to their sons or take their daughters for your sons, 4because they will turn your sons away from me to worship other gods. Then the Lord's anger will burn against you, and he will swiftly destroy you. 5Instead, this is what you are to do to them: tear down their altars, smash their sacred pillars, cut down their Asherah poles, and burn their carved images. 6For you are a holy people belonging to the Lord your God. The Lord your God has chosen you to be his own possession out of all the peoples on the face of the earth. 7"The Lord had his heart set on you and chose you, not because you were more numerous than all peoples, for you were the fewest of all peoples. 8But because the Lord loved you and kept the oath he swore to your fathers, he brought you out with a strong hand and

redeemed you from the place of slavery, from the power of Pharaoh king of Egypt."

What Jonah leaves out as he quotes Exodus 34:6-7 is telling: "But he will not leave the guilty unpunished..." Jonah seems to be accusing God of being faithless toward his own Word. But what we see is that God's desire is for sinful, fallen image bearers to turn from their "evil ways." God does not revel in the destruction of sinners as He does in the redemption of sinners.

4:3-4

Jonah would rather die than live in a world where evildoers go free—off without consequence. We also see that Jonah is so arrogant and full of pride that he does not even answer the Lord's question. What a kindness it is that the Lord does not destroy him on the spot.

ACT 4, SCENE 2: JONAH'S TWISTED HEART (VV.5-7)

4:5

Jonah is pretty twisted! He positions himself outside the city for protection from what he hopes will be a fireworks show to remember. Jonah wants to watch God unleash a fiery fury down upon Nineveh just as with Sodom and Gomorrah (Genesis 19). He wants to pull up a lawn chair, grab a bag of popcorn, and watch the Lord rain down a furious judgment.

4:6-7

The Lord responds to Jonah's hatred by heaping kindness after kindness after kindness upon his head. This last kindness is meant to snap Jonah out of his ironic, sinful rage. We again see the Lord's heart as He remains committed to the process of making Jonah holy—all the way to the day of resurrection.

The Lord shades Jonah by providing a miraculous plant, probably some form of fast-growing vine, which is meant to be an object lesson for Jonah—an object lesson that seemingly goes right over his hot head. The Lord then appoints a worm to destroy the vine in order to set up Jonah to somehow grasp the false vision of his moral superiority. This becomes more apparent as the Lord unveils his intention in 4:10-11.

ACT 4, SCENE 3: JONAH'S FICKLE HEART (VV.8-9)

4:8-9

The Lord carries the object lesson further: Jonah becomes even more furious with the Lord as his head begins to smolder under the sun. Jonah fails to connect the irony that he wishes God would burn the Ninevites alive, but himself is quite angry with God because of his sunburn. The irony is thick enough to cut with a knife!

OBEY THE WORD OF THE LORD

Have you noticed how everybody and everything in this story obeys the Lord except for Jonah?

- The ocean obeys the Lord.
- The wind obeys the Lord.
- They cast lots, and it dutifully fell on Jonah as the Lord intended.
- The sailors show obedience as fear overcomes them. They throw Jonah overboard, and the seas cease to rage, just as the prophet of God testified.
- The fish obeys by swallowing Jonah just at the appointed time, and he promptly spits him out at just the appointed time.
- The Ninevites repent and obey at the mere preaching of the Word of the Lord through Jonah.
- The plant obeys God and grows and withers at the appointed time (4:6).
- The worm obeys by attacking the plant (4:7).
- The sun and east wind obey God when they join forces to scorch Jonah's head (4:8).

Everybody and everything obeys God's sovereign rule except for Jonah.

ACT 4 — SCENE 4: THE LORD'S MERCIFUL HEART (VV.10-11)

4:10-11

The Lord's heart does not lean toward punishment but toward pardon. In chapter two Jonah confesses that the Lord had thrown him "into the heart of the sea," but we see in actuality this whole voyage has been concerned with throwing Jonah more so into the heart of THE LORD. It has been an expedition into God's merciful nature.

The Lord is a Lord who delights to save the broken, wicked, defenseless, unclean, the drunkards, the adulterer, the wife beaters, the rapists, and the sexually immoral. We see in 1:2 that the Lord does not see the Ninevites as innocent. Therefore, what God means by saying the Ninevites could not "distinguish between their right and their left" is that they have lost their way morally. They couldn't tell right from wrong. And He cares greatly for these many souls, trapped in a pattern, a vicious cycle of generation after generation of "evil ways." The Lord is intimately and personally connected to His creation.

What's the point? Even here at the end of the book, it ends awkwardly with Jonah still baffled and perplexed by God's mercy to rebels. He still does not get it. God's mercy is so overwhelming that it is incomprehensible to finite creatures like Jonah, you, and me. God's mercy and grace is so stupefyingly merciful and gracious that we can't even accept it. It's so big and swallowing that we seek to reject it, and even in that state, His mercies pursue us still. God cannot help Himself. It is what He's like. He is relentless in pursuing sinners. Jonah said it himself: "I knew that you are a gracious and compassionate God, slow to anger, abounding in faithful love, and one who relents from sending disaster."

JESUS: THE TRUE, BETTER, AND GREATER JONAH

Jesus, too, was once banished from the Lord's presence (Matt 27:45-50 and Psalm 22), but He was not guilty of sin! Jonah was driven out because of his sin, but Jesus was driven out on behalf of sinners. He Himself was sinless!

Consider the following parallels between Jesus and Jonah:

- Jonah hates Nineveh and responds with anger < Jesus loved Jerusalem and wept over her
- Jonah delighted to preach destruction to Nineveh < Jesus delighted to preach forgiveness through His blood
- Jonah is full of sin, yet the Father mercifully spared him < Jesus had no sin, yet died like a sinner to deliver sinners like you and me.
- Jonah was in the belly of the fish and figuratively arose from the heart of the seas after three days, and thus was a foreshadowing < Jesus got up out of the belly of the earth after three days and was the substance.

BIBLIOGRAPHY

Alexander, T. Desmond. *Obadiah, Jonah, and Micah.* Tyndale Old Testament Commentaries. Downer's Grove: IVP Academic, 1988.

Belibtreu, Erika. "Grisly Assyrian Record of Torture and Death." *Biblical Archaeological Review 17, no. 1* (Jan/Feb: 1993): 52-61.

Cardoso, Renato. "Who was Sennecherib?" (video), August 5, 2010. https://www.youtube.com/watch?v=TR_poifNJYU&feature=youtu.be&t=138.

Dever, Mark. "Can You Run from God? The Message of Jonah." Capitol Hill Baptist sermon, Washingon, D.C., September 28, 2003. Audio.

Dooley, Adam. "Jonah: A Preaching Prophet" (video of lecture). Southwestern Baptist Theological Seminary, Expository Preaching Workshop 2011, February 28, 2011. http://media.swbts.edu/item/489/jonah-a-preaching-prophet.

Estelle, Bryan D. *Salvation through Mercy and Judgement: The Gospel According to Jonah.* Phillipsburg: P&R Publishing, 2005.

Ferguson, Sinclair. *Man Overboard! The Story of Jonah.* Edinburgh: The Banner of Truth Press, 2008.

Mackie, Tim. "1. Running From Your Life – Amazing Jonah – Time Mackie (The Bible Project)" (video). Door of Hope sermon, Portland, OR, September 1, 2013. https://www.youtube.com/watch?list=PLDVooRp5-IwdoJUykoj6Rvkw_s_jEg2Rf.&v=ah1RRqQg2fM.
—. "2. Asleep at the Wheel – Amazing Jonah – Tim Mackie (The Bible Project)" (video), Door of Hope sermon, Portland, OR, August 11, 2013. https://www.youtube.com/watch?v=-MumrlFaakD4.

—. "3. A Severe Mercy – Amazing Jonah – Tim Mackie (The Bible Project)" (video), Door of Hope sermon, Portland, OR, August 18, 2013. https://www.youtube.com/watch?v=twFhijg8lQs.

—. "4. Thrones and Ashes – Amazing Jonah – Tim Mackie (The Bible Project)" (video), Door of Hope sermon, Portland, OR, August 25, 2013. https://www.youtube.com/watch?v=7AgpZwzPyPI.

Mahaney, C.J. "A Scandalous Mercy: Jonah 2." Sovereign Grace Church of Louisville sermon, Jeffersontown, KY, October 16, 2016. https://www.sgclouisville.org/mediaPlayer/#/sermonaudio/215. Media Player.

—. "A Tender Mercy: Jonah 4." Sovereign Grace Church of Louisville sermon, Jeffersontown, KY, December 4, 2016. https://www.sgclouisville.org/mediaPlayer/#/sermonaudio/222. Media Player.

Mark, Joshua J. "Assyrian Warfare." Ancient History Encyclopedia. May 2, 2018. https://www.ancient.eu/Assyrian_Warfare/.

Piper, John. "The Education of a Prophet: Jonah." Bethlehem Baptist Church sermon, Minneapolis, Minnesota, May 3, 1981. https://www.desiringgod.org/messages/the-education-of-a-prophet-jonah.

—. "Cry of Distress and Voice of Thanks: The Prayer of Jonah." Bethlehem Baptist Church sermon, Minneapolis, Minnesota, November 21, 1982. https://www.desiringgod.org/messages/cry-of-distress-and-voice-of-thanks.

—. "Should Not I Pity that Great City…Minneapolis?" Bethlehem Baptist Church sermon, Minneapolis, Minnesota, June 7, 1992. https://www.desiringgod.org/messages/should-not-i-pity-that-great-city-minneapolis.

BIBLIOGRAPHY

"Ripping Open Pregnant Women." Claude Mariottini. Dr. Claude Mariottini – Professor of Old Testament. June 19, 2014.

Smith, Collin S. Jonah: Navigating A God-Centered Life. Geanies House, Scotland: Christian Focus Publications, 2012.

Sproul, R.C. *The Reformation Study Bible.* Orlando: Ligonier Ministries, 2005.

Timmer, Daniel C. *A Gracious and Compassionate God: Mission, Salvation, and Spirituality in the Book of Jonah.* Downers Grove: IVP Academic, 2011.

Wilson, Doug. "Surveying the Text: Jonah." Christ Church sermon, Moscow, ID, June 14, 2015. https://www.christkirk.com/sermon/surveying-text-jonah/.

NOTES

NOTES

NOTES

NOTES

NOTES

NOTES

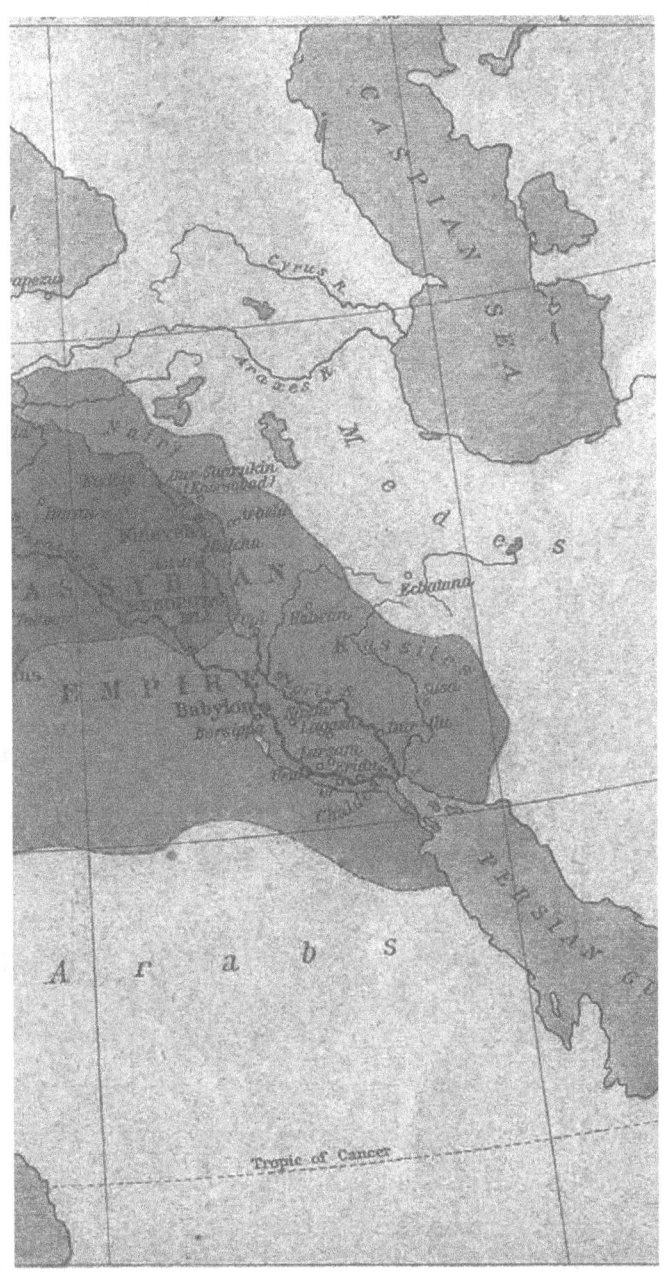

www.ingramcontent.com/pod-product-compliance
Lightning Source LLC
Chambersburg PA
CBHW050336120526
44592CB00014B/2207